Name ___________

Draw a Picture

I Can...

- [ ] use a Capital Letter
  The cat is big.
- [ ] use spaces
- [ ] sound out words
  d-o-g = dog
- [ ] use a Period .
- [ ] Draw a picture

He is having fun, running
under the sun with his
new toy gun.

fun	gun	run	sun
楽しい	銃	走る	太陽

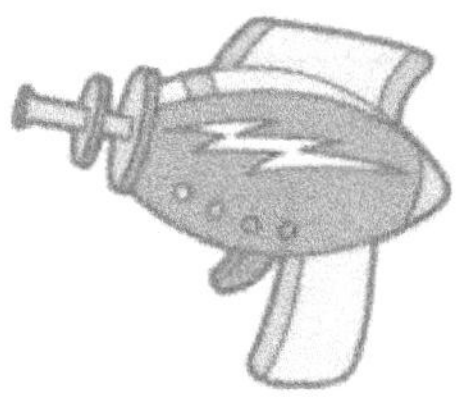

Name: ____________________ Date: ____________________

Today is: Monday Tuesday Wednesday Thursday Friday

Direction: Trace and read the sentences.

bag	rag	tag	wag

バッグ	ぼろ	鬼ごっこ	振る

He has many bags.

I see a rag.

I see a tag.

Its tail is wagging.

My Sight Word List

a	in	said
and	is	see
away	it	the
big	jump	three
blue	little	to
can	look	two
come	make	up
down	me	we
find	my	where
for	not	yellow
funny	one	you
go	day	
help	play	
here	red	
I	run	

Name: ______________________ Date: ______________________

Today is: Monday | Tuesday | Wednesday | Thursday | Friday

Direction: Trace and read the sentences.

fun	gun	run	sun
	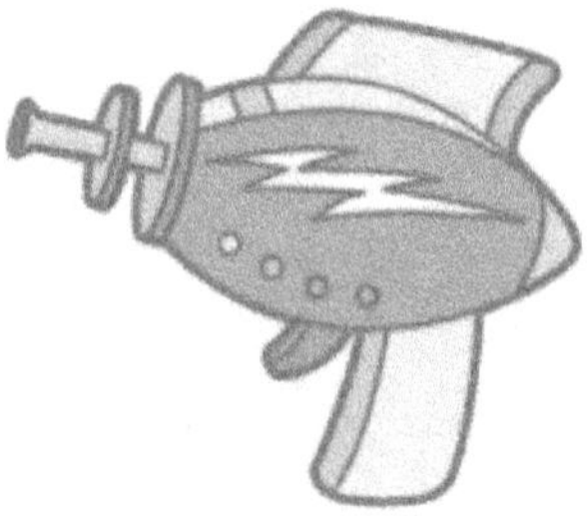		
楽しい	銃	走る	太陽

They are having fun.

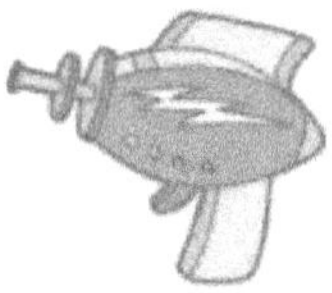

He has a gun.

The bear is running.

The sun is smiling.

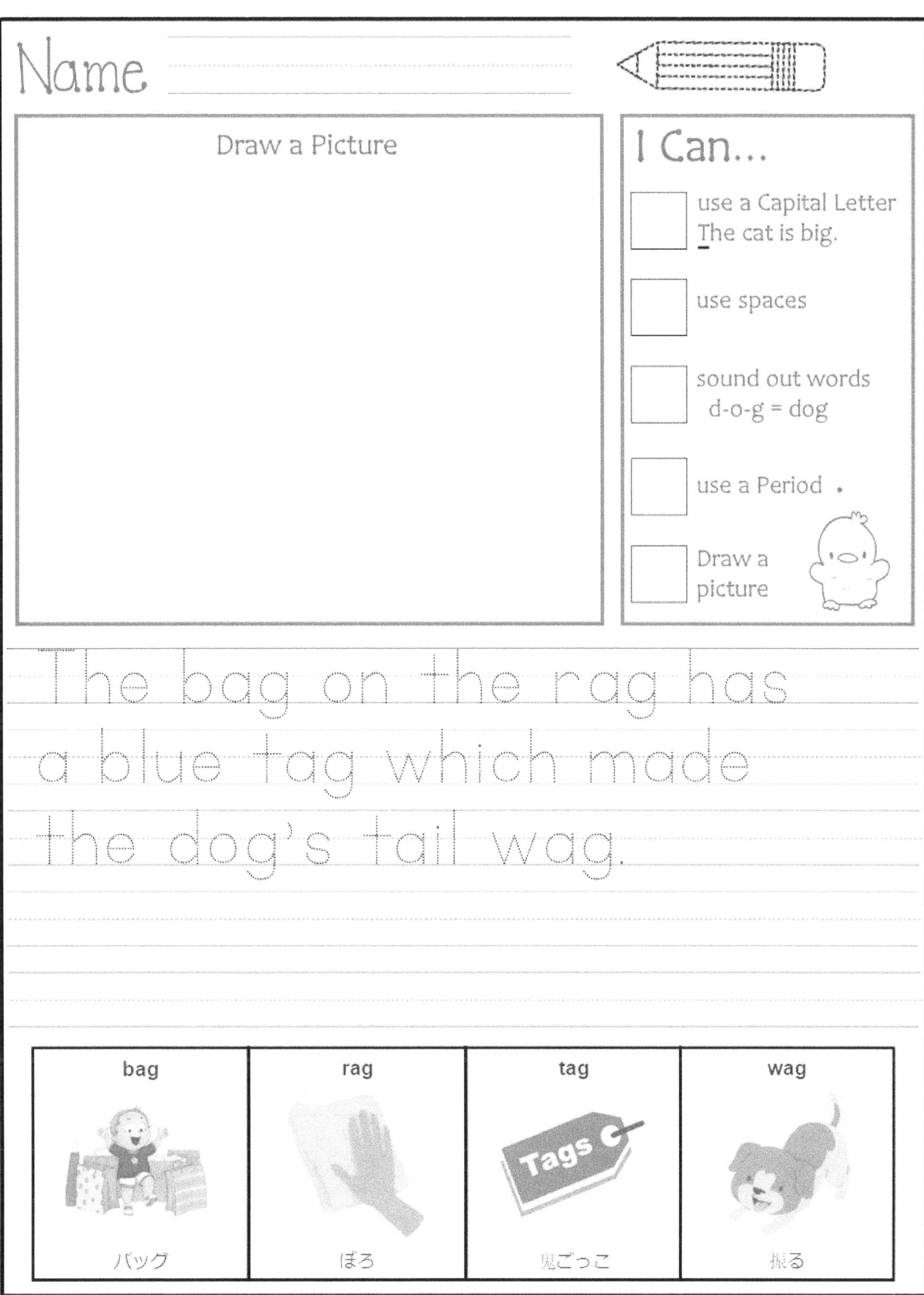

Name
Draw a Picture
I Can...
use a Capital Letter
The cat is big.
use spaces
sound out words
d-o-g = dog
use a Period .
Draw a picture
The bag on the rag has a blue tag which made the dog's tail wag.
bag
rag
tag
wag
バッグ
ぼろ
鬼ごっこ
振る

Name: ____________________ Date: ____________________

Today is: Monday Tuesday Wednesday Thursday Friday

Direction: Trace and read the sentences.

can	man	pan	van

缶	おとこ	パン	バン

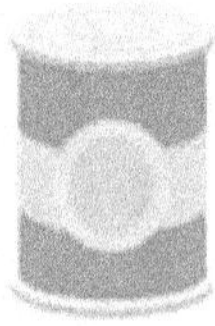

I see a can of soda.

The man is happy.

The pan is dirty.

I see a big van.

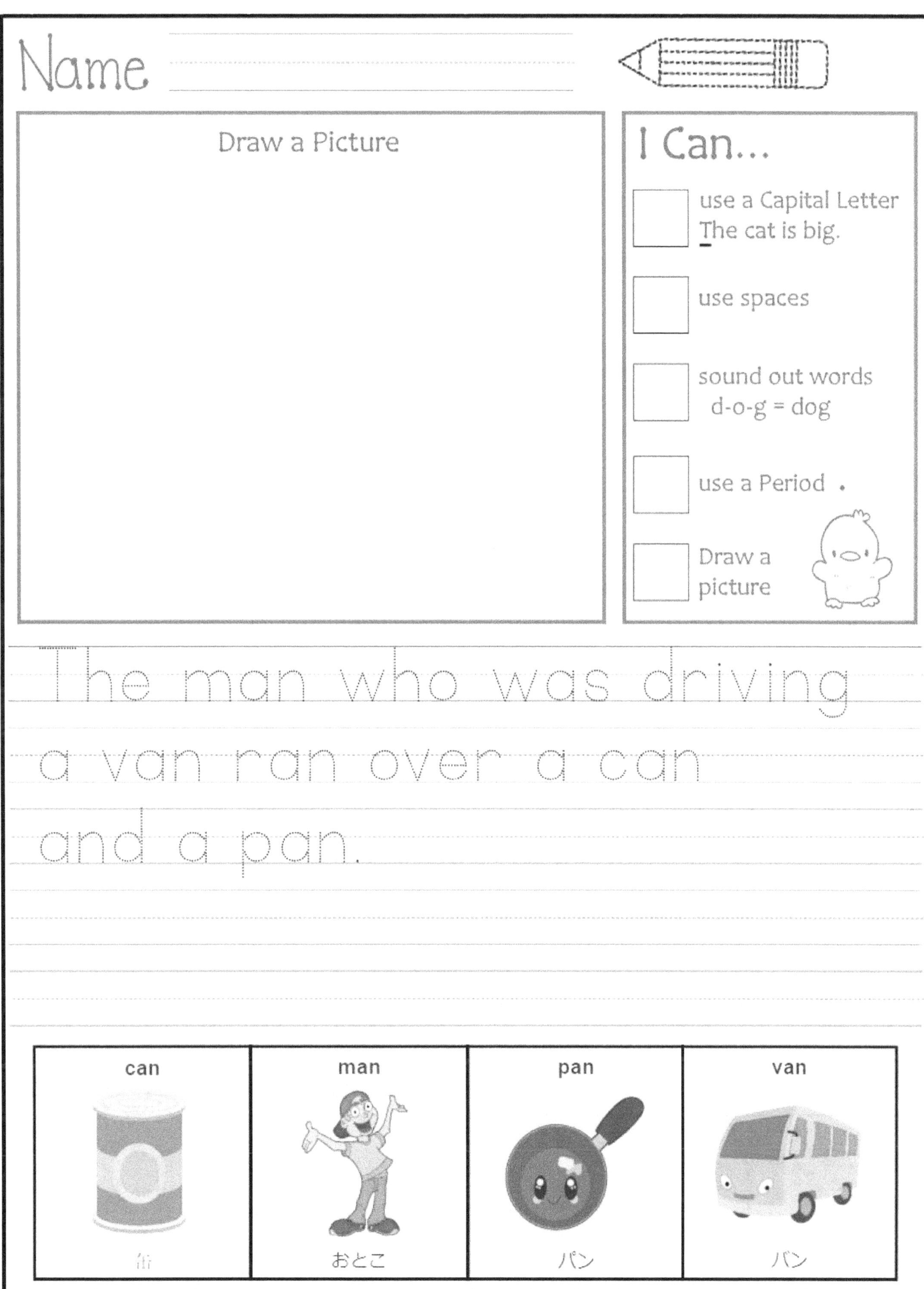

Name

Draw a Picture

I Can...
☐ use a Capital Letter
The cat is big.

☐ use spaces

☐ sound out words
d-o-g = dog

☐ use a Period .

☐ Draw a picture

The man who was driving
a van ran over a can
and a pan.

can
缶

man
おとこ

pan
パン

van
バン

Name: _________________________ Date: _______________

Today is: [Monday] [Tuesday] [Wednesday]
[Thursday] [Friday]

Direction: Trace and read the sentences.

cut	gut	hut	nut
切る	腸	小屋	ナット

He cut his nails.

He has a gut.

This is a small hut.

It is holding a nut.

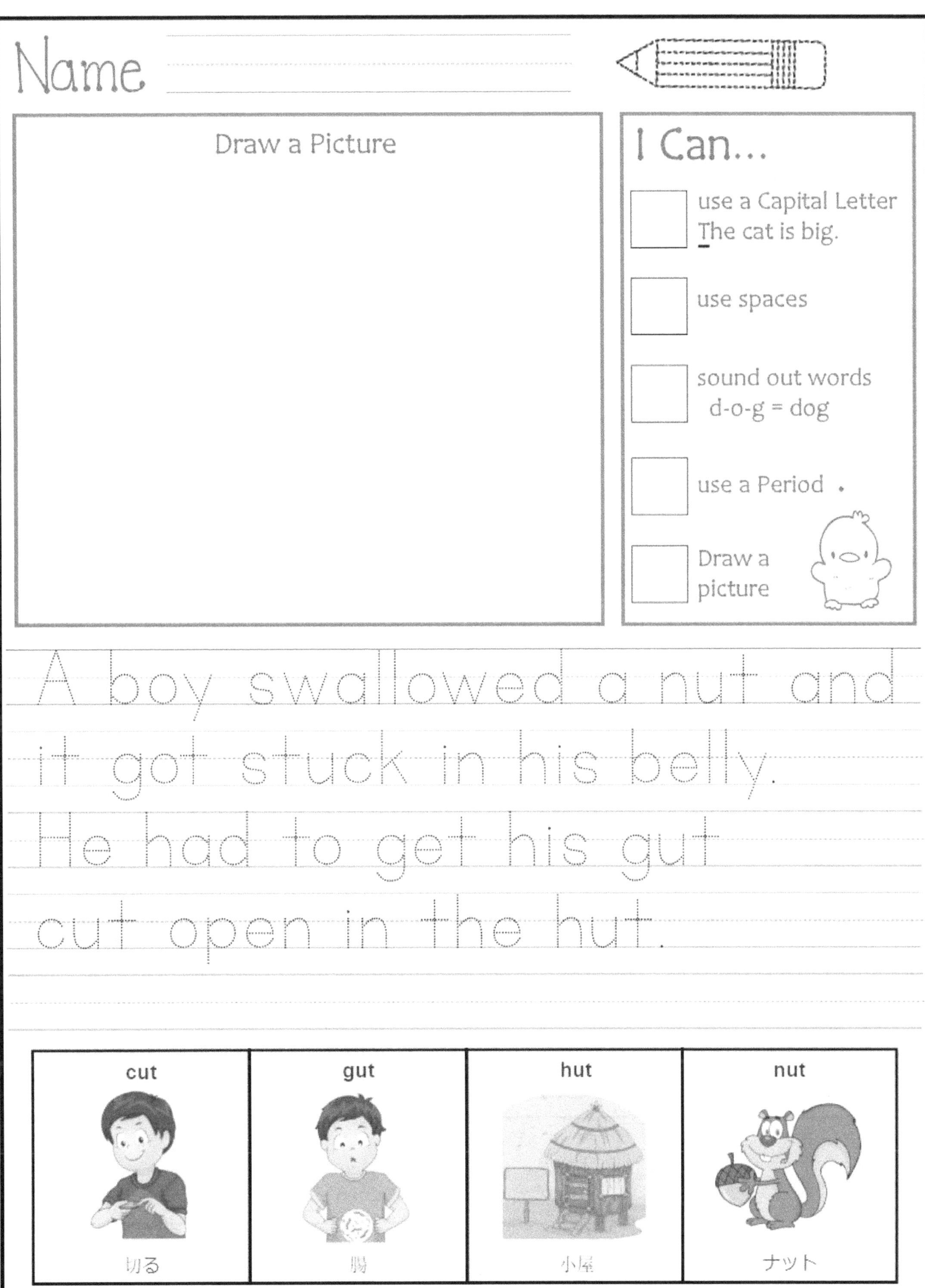

A boy swallowed a nut and
it got stuck in his belly.
He had to get his gut
cut open in the hut.

Name: ____________________ Date: ____________________

Today is: Monday | Tuesday | Wednesday | Thursday | Friday

Direction: Trace and read the sentences.

fat

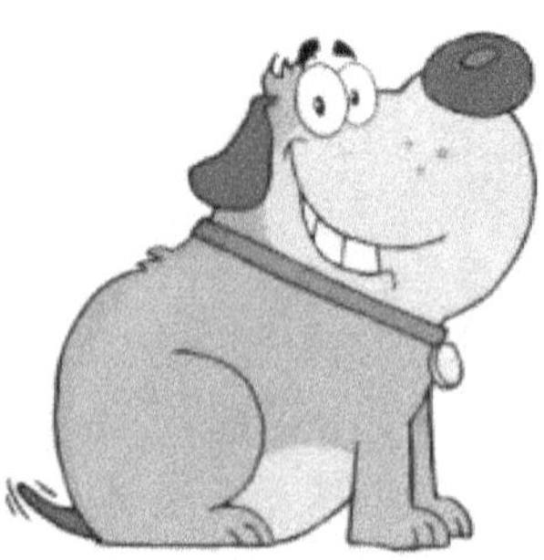

太い

cat

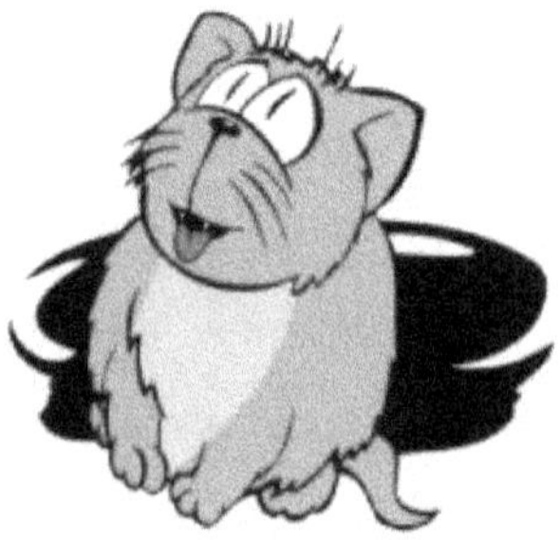

ネコ

hat

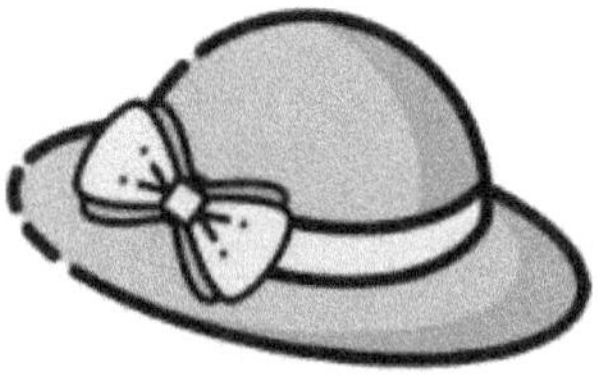

帽子

mat

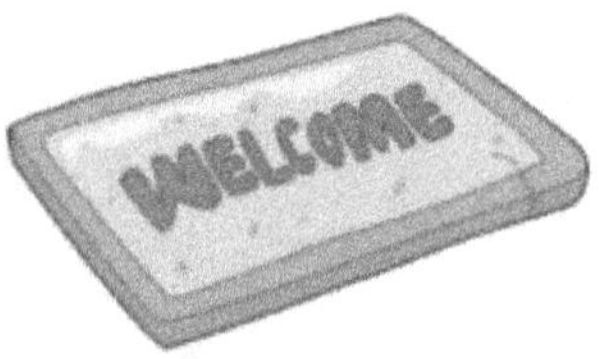

マット

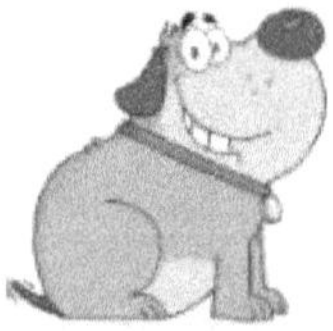

I see a fat dog.

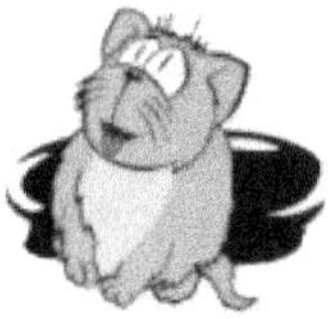

This is my little cat.

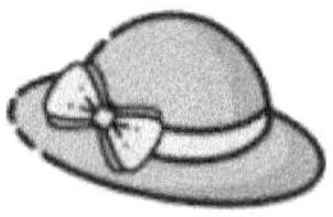

I like this hat.

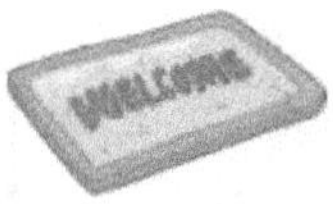

I see a big mat.

The fat cat laid on the mat that was a hat pattern.

Name: _________________ Date: _______

Today is: [Monday] [Tuesday] [Wednesday]
[Thursday] [Friday]

Direction: Trace and read the sentences.

cab	lab	tab	crab
タクシー	ラボ	タブ	カニ

The cab is fast.

The lab is exciting.

The tab is long.

We found a crab.

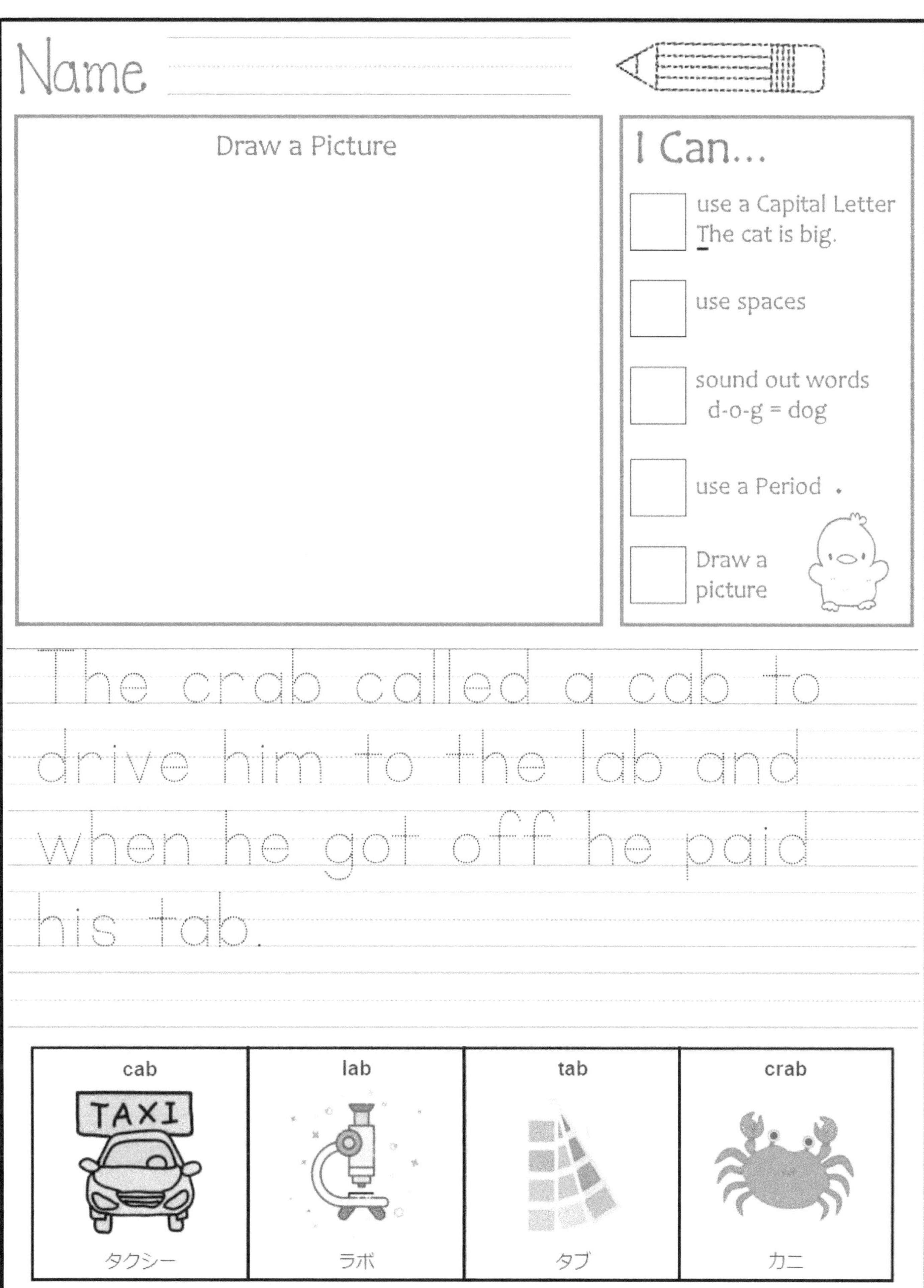

Name

Draw a Picture

I Can...
use a Capital Letter
The cat is big.
use spaces
sound out words
d-o-g = dog
use a Period .
Draw a
picture

The crab called a cab to
drive him to the lab and
when he got off he paid
his tab.

cab
TAXI
タクシー

lab
ラボ

tab
タブ

crab
カニ

Name: ____________________ Date: ____________________

Today is: Monday Tuesday Wednesday Thursday Friday

Direction: Trace and read the sentences.

ham	jam	ram	clam

ハム	混雑する	羊	シェル

I like to eat ham.

We like to eat jam.

The ram is big.

The clam is pretty.

Draw a Picture

I Can...

use a Capital Letter
The cat is big.

use spaces

sound out words
d-o-g = dog

use a Period .

Draw a
picture

The clam gave the ram ham. Then the ram gave the clam jam.

ham	jam	ram	clam
ハム	混雑する	羊	シェル

Name: ___________________ Date: ___________

Today is: [Monday] [Tuesday] [Wednesday]
[Thursday] [Friday]

Direction: Trace and read the sentences.

bed	led	red	wed
ベッド	主導	赤	結婚式

This is my little bed.

He led us to safety.

The apple is red.

He asks her to wed.

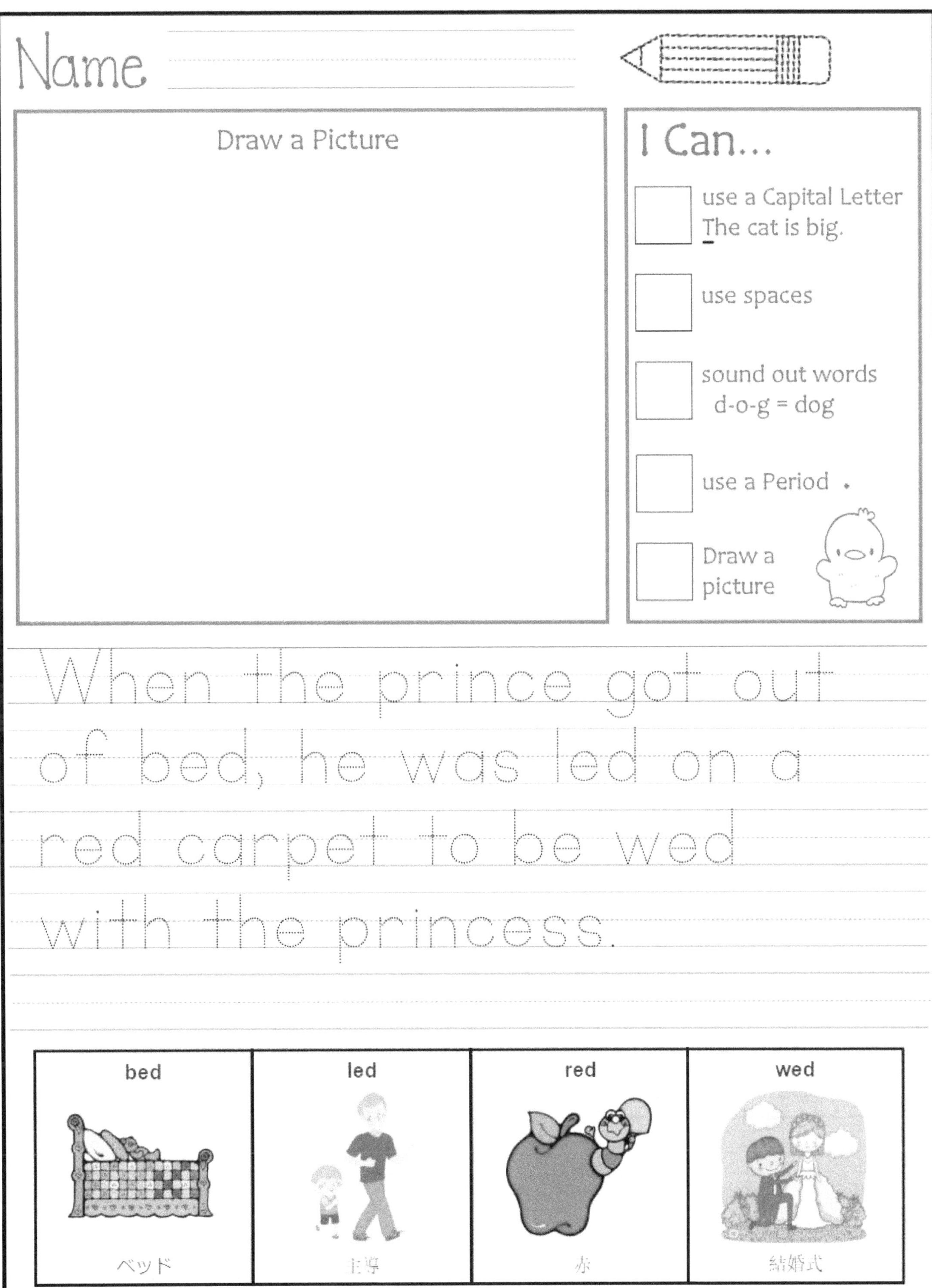

When the prince got out of bed, he was led on a red carpet to be wed with the princess.

Name: _______________________ Date: _______________

Today is: [Monday] [Tuesday] [Wednesday]
[Thursday] [Friday]

Direction: Trace and read the sentences.

bad	dad	mad	sad
悪い	パパ	狂った	悲しい

This apple is bad.

My dad is very kind.

The reindeer is mad.

The little cat is sad.

Name ____________________

Draw a Picture

I Can...

- [ ] use a Capital Letter
  The cat is big.

- [ ] use spaces

- [ ] sound out words
  d-o-g = dog

- [ ] use a Period .

- [ ] Draw a picture

I was bad so my dad
got mad and now
I am so sad.

bad	dad	mad	sad
悪い	パパ	狂った	悲しい

Name: _________________ Date: _________

Today is: [Monday] [Tuesday] [Wednesday]
[Thursday] [Friday]

Direction: Trace and read the sentences.

den	hen	pen	ten
デン	編	厩舎	十

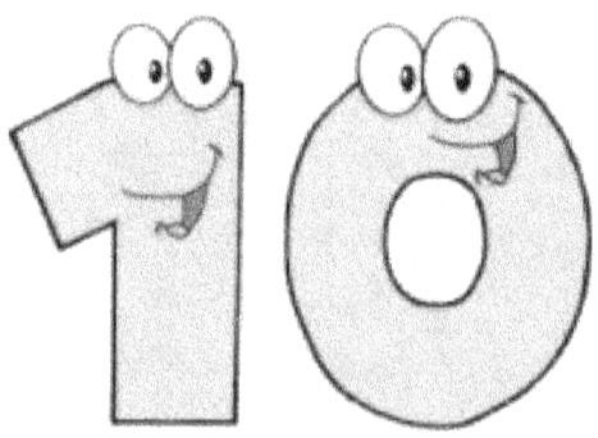

It is a den.

The hens lay eggs.

She has a good pen.

The ten is smiling.

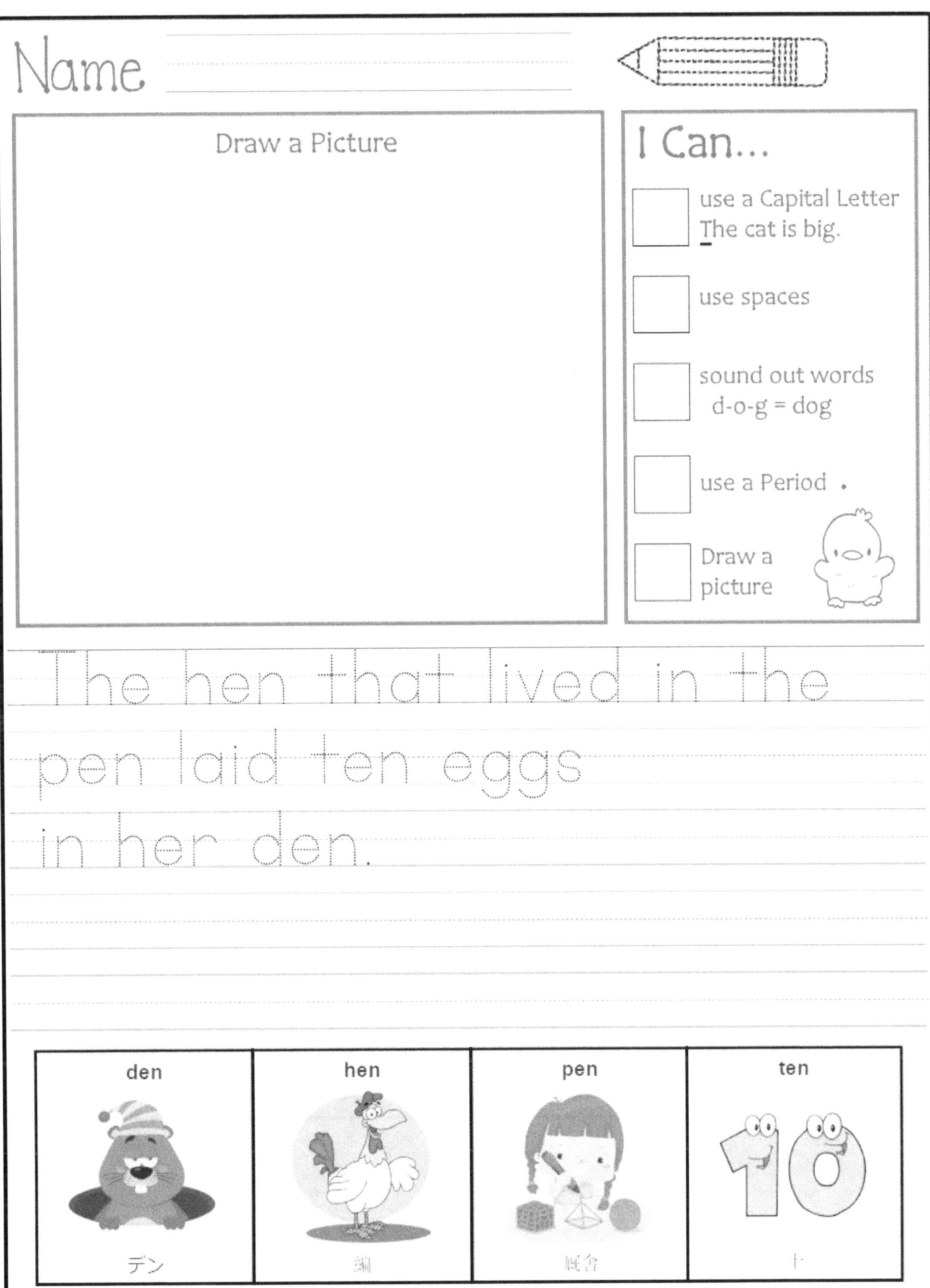

Name
Draw a Picture
I Can...
use a Capital Letter
The cat is big.
use spaces
sound out words
d-o-g = dog
use a Period .
Draw a picture
The hen that lived in the pen laid ten eggs in her den.
den
デン
hen
編
pen
厩舎
ten
十

Name: _______________________ Date: _____________

Today is: Monday Tuesday Wednesday
           Thursday Friday

Direction: Trace and read the sentences.

gum	mum	sum	drum
グミ	お母さん	和	ドラム

I like to chew gum.

My mum is kind!

I can do a sum!

The drum is big.

Name

Draw a Picture

I Can...

- [ ] use a Capital Letter
  The cat is big.
- [ ] use spaces
- [ ] sound out words
  d-o-g = dog
- [ ] use a Period .
- [ ] Draw a picture

Mum was chewing gum while figuring out the sum of the drum's price.

gum	mum	sum	drum
グミ	お母さん	和	ドラム

Name: _______________ Date: _______________

Today is: [Monday] [Tuesday] [Wednesday]
[Thursday] [Friday]

Direction: Trace and read the sentences.

bid	hid	kid	lid
入札	隠す	キッド	蓋

He likes to bid.

He is hiding.

The kid like to play.

I see a lid.

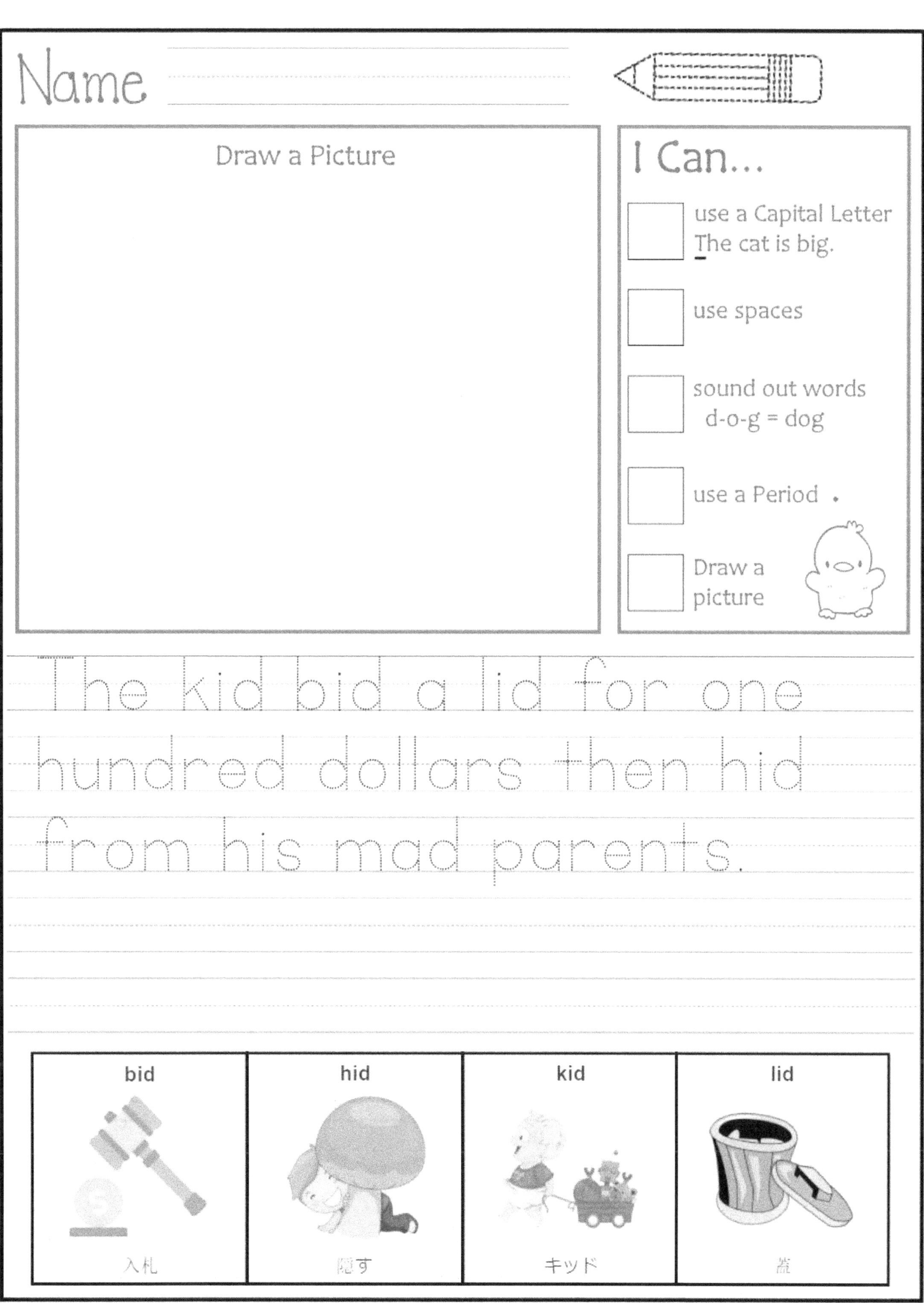

Name

Draw a Picture

I Can...

use a Capital Letter
The cat is big.

use spaces

sound out words
d-o-g = dog

use a Period .

Draw a
picture

The kid bid a lid for one
hundred dollars then hid
from his mad parents.

bid
入札

hid
隠す

kid
キッド

lid
蓋

Name: ____________________ Date: ____________________

Today is: Monday | Tuesday | Wednesday | Thursday | Friday

Direction: Trace and read the sentences.

big	dig	pig	wig

大きい	掘る	豚	かつら

That is a big pencil.

He will dig up a hole.

The pig is fat.

She puts on a wig.

Draw a Picture

I Can...

- [ ] use a Capital Letter
  The cat is big.

- [ ] use spaces

- [ ] sound out words
  d-o-g = dog

- [ ] use a Period .

- [ ] Draw a picture

The big pig went to dig in the mud for his wig.

big	dig	pig	wig
大きい	掘る	豚	かつら

Name: _______________ Date: _______________

Today is: [Monday] [Tuesday] [Wednesday]
[Thursday] [Friday]

Direction: Trace and read the sentences.

bin	fin	pin	win
置き場	フィン	ピン	勝つ

It is a recycle bin.

The shark has a fin.

The pin is pointy.

He won the match.

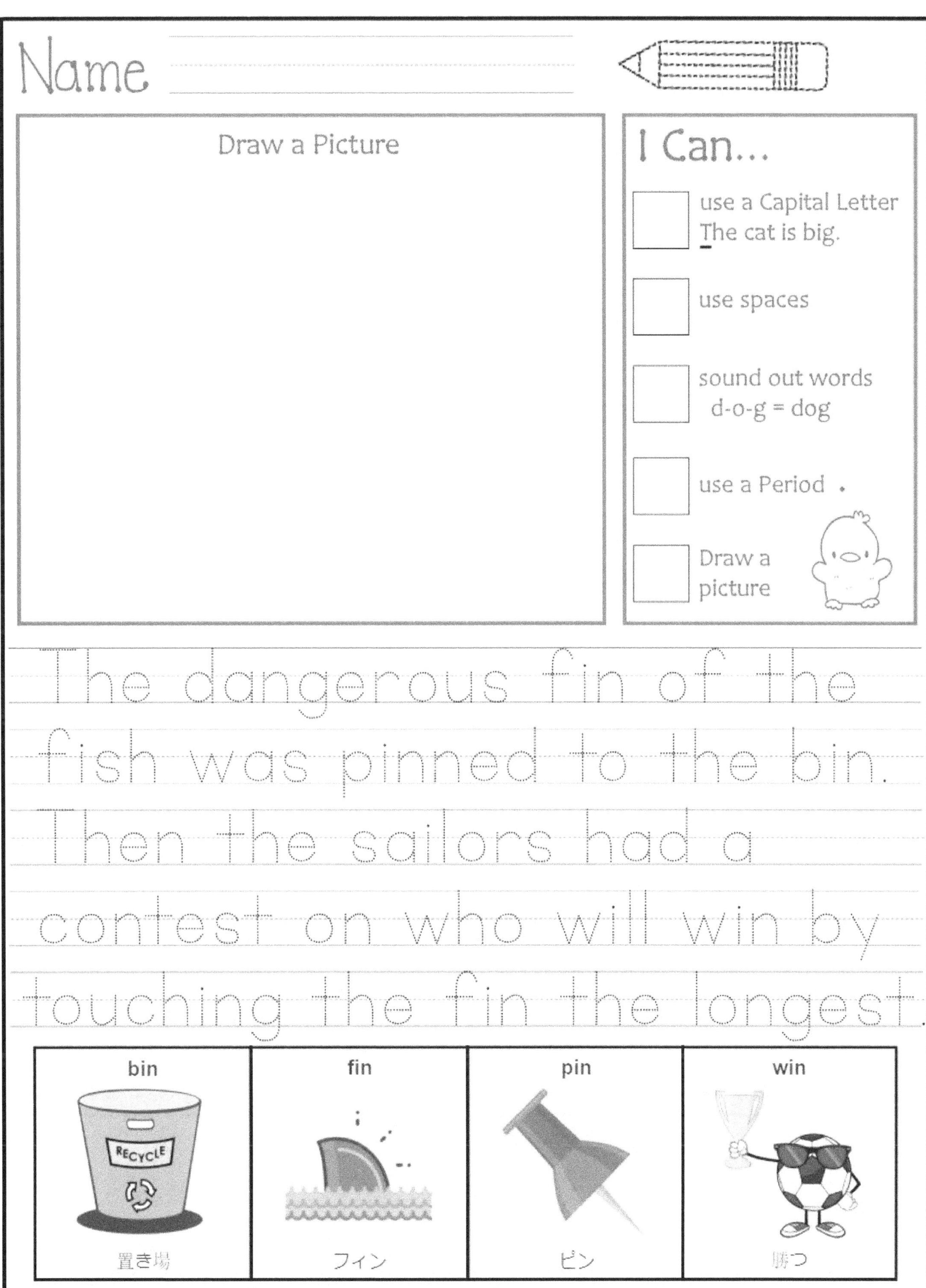

Name

Draw a Picture

I Can...

use a Capital Letter
The cat is big.

use spaces

sound out words
d-o-g = dog

use a Period .

Draw a picture

The dangerous fin of the
fish was pinned to the bin.
Then the sailors had a
contest on who will win by
touching the fin the longest.

bin
RECYCLE
置き場

fin
フィン

pin
ピン

win
勝つ

Name: ____________________ Date: ____________________

Today is: Monday Tuesday Wednesday Thursday Friday

Direction: Trace and read the sentences.

hip	lip	nip	sip

ヒップ	唇	ニップ	ドリンク

This is my hip.

Her lips are red.

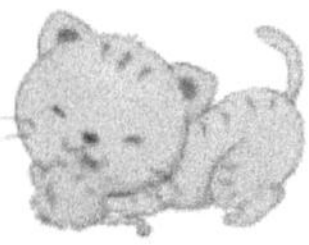

It is nipping its toy.

She is sipping.

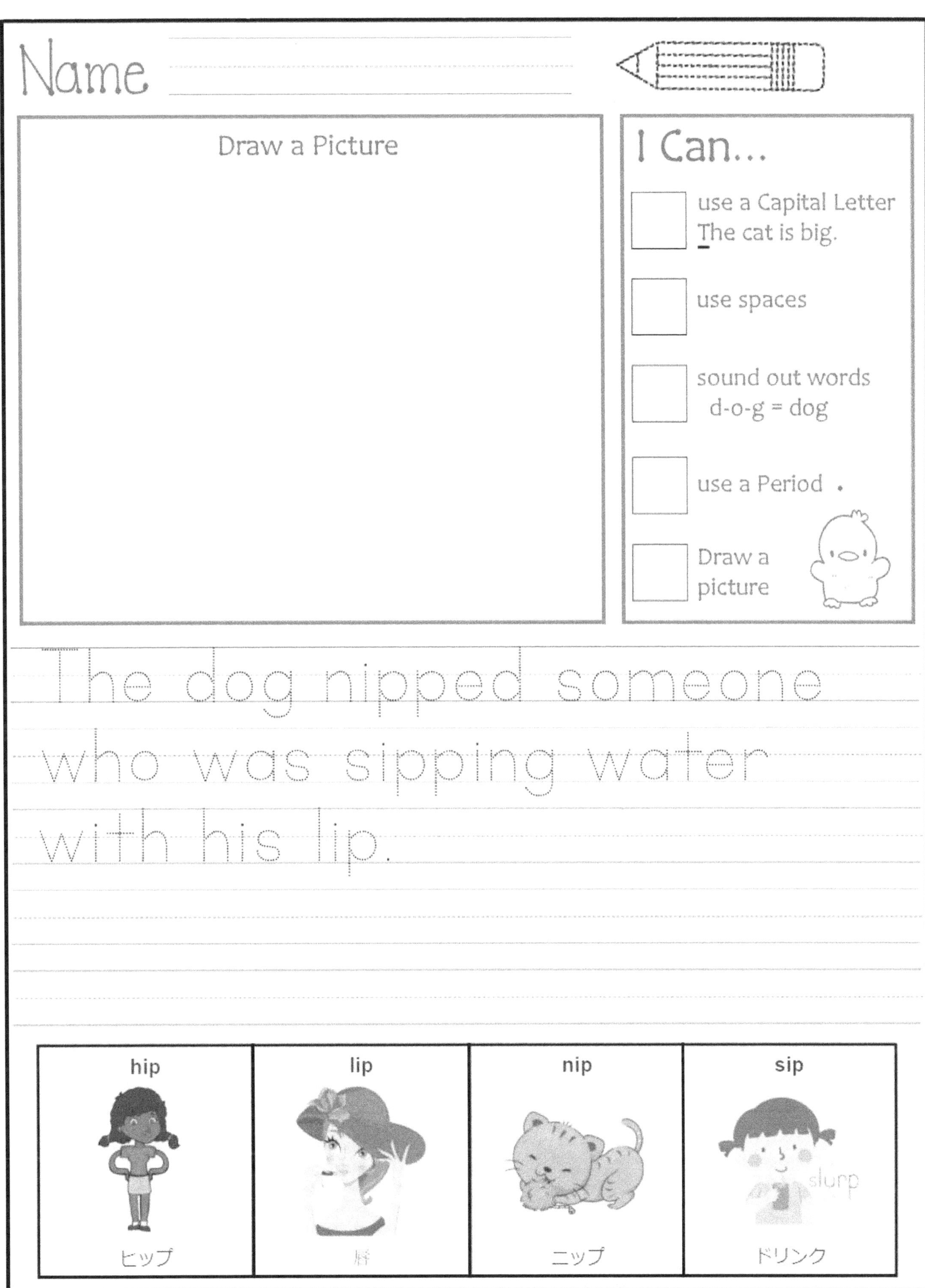

Name
Draw a Picture
I Can...
use a Capital Letter
The cat is big.
use spaces
sound out words
d-o-g = dog
use a Period .
Draw a picture
The dog nipped someone who was sipping water with his lip.
hip
lip
nip
sip
ヒップ
唇
ニップ
ドリンク
slurp

Name: ____________________ Date: ____________________

Today is: Monday Tuesday Wednesday Thursday Friday

Direction: Trace and read the sentences.

fit	hit	kit	sit
		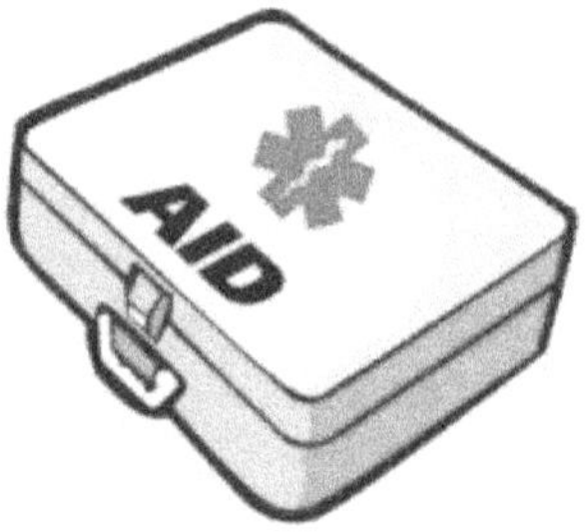	
フィット	ヒット	キット	座る

It is perfectly fit.

They hit each other.

That is a safety kit.

He is sitting.

Name ____________________

Draw a Picture

I Can...

- [ ] use a Capital Letter
  The cat is big.
- [ ] use spaces
- [ ] sound out words
  d-o-g = dog
- [ ] use a Period .
- [ ] Draw a picture

The fit doctor sat then was hit by a kit.

fit	hit	kit	sit
フィット	ヒット	キット	座る

Name: ____________________ Date: ____________________

Today is: Monday Tuesday Wednesday Thursday Friday

Direction: Trace and read the sentences.

cob	job	rob	sob

コーン	ジョブ	奪う	泣く

I ate corn on the cob.

This is my job.

He is robbing.

The girl is sobbing.

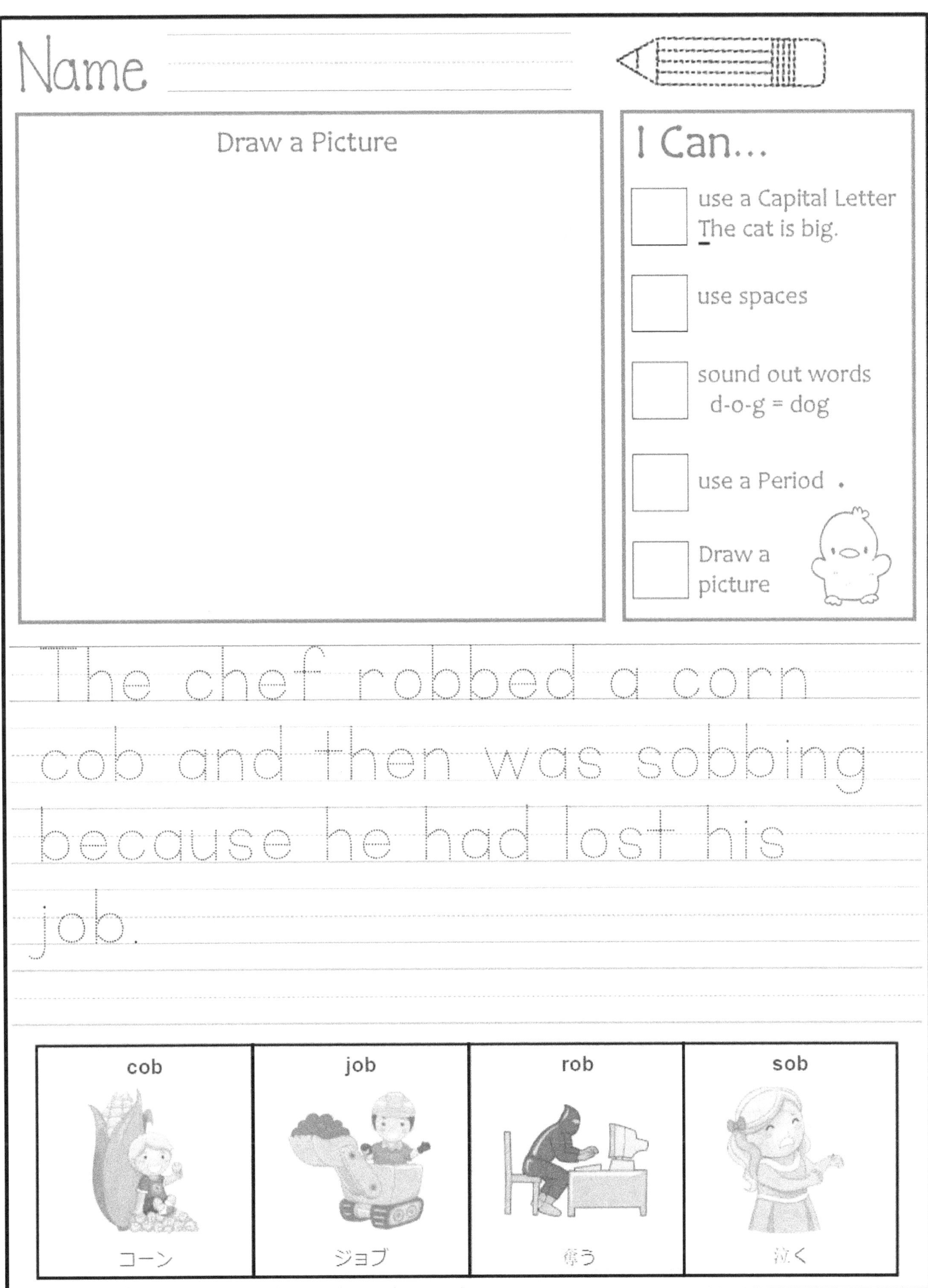

Name
Draw a Picture
I Can...
use a Capital Letter
The cat is big.
use spaces
sound out words
d-o-g = dog
use a Period .
Draw a
picture
The chef robbed a corn
cob and then was sobbing
because he had lost his
job.
cob
job
rob
sob
コーン
ジョブ
奪う
泣く

Name: _________________ Date: __________

Today is: [Monday] [Tuesday] [Wednesday]
[Thursday] [Friday]

Direction: Trace and read the sentences.

dog	hog	jog	log
犬	豚	ジョギング	木材

The dog is thrilled.

The hog is big.

She is jogging.

The log is small.

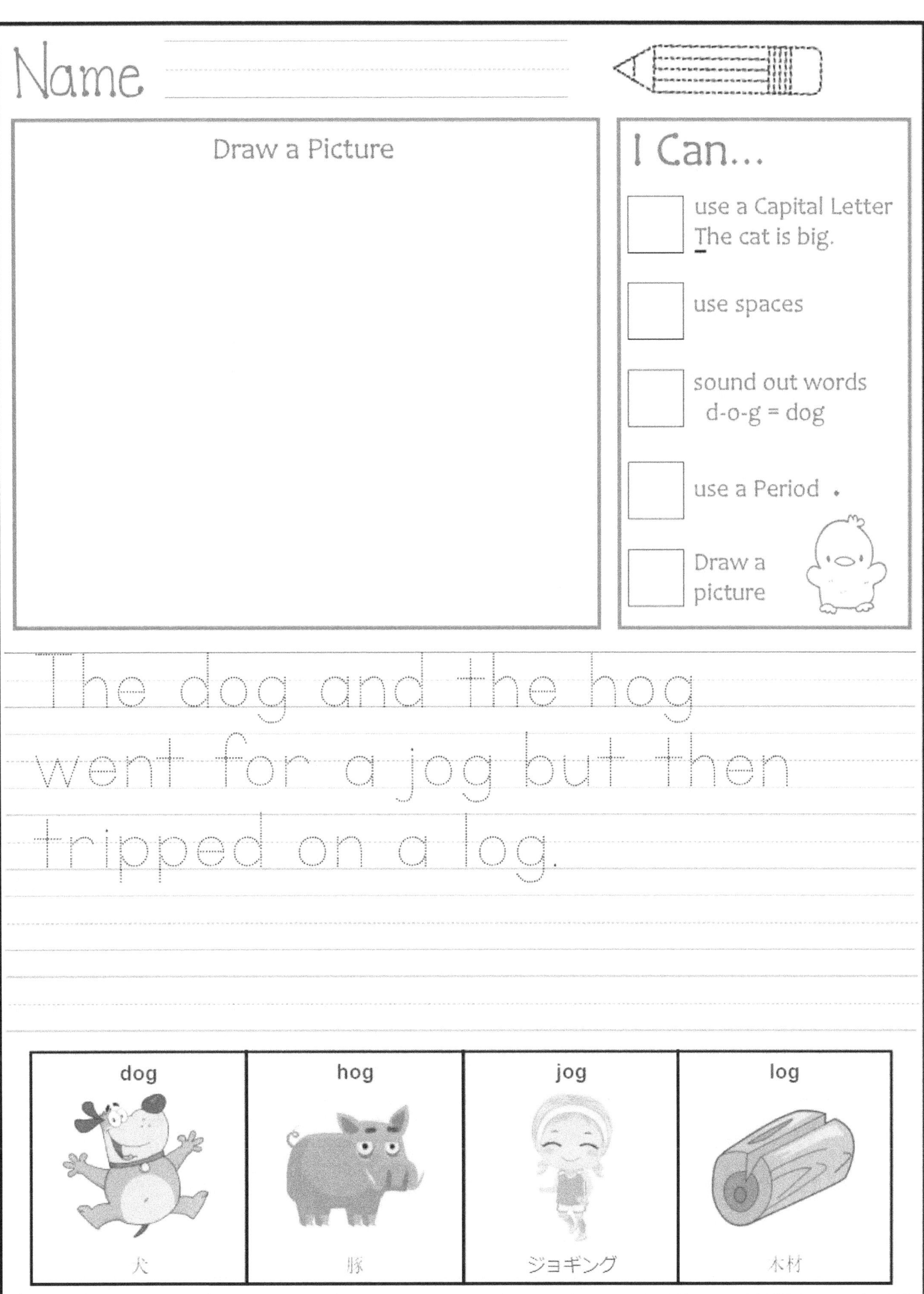

Name
Draw a Picture
I Can...
use a Capital Letter
The cat is big.
use spaces
sound out words
d-o-g = dog
use a Period .
Draw a picture
The dog and the hog went for a jog but then tripped on a log.
dog
hog
jog
log
犬
豚
ジョギング
木材

Name: _________________ Date: _______

Today is: [Monday] [Tuesday] [Wednesday]
[Thursday] [Friday]

Direction: Trace and read the sentences.

bug	hug	jug	mug
バグ	抱擁	水差し	マグ

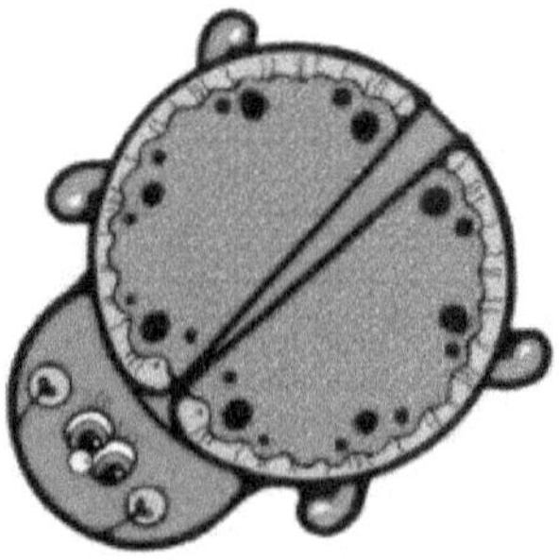

The bug is colorful.

She is hugging.

The jug has milk in it.

He has a mug.

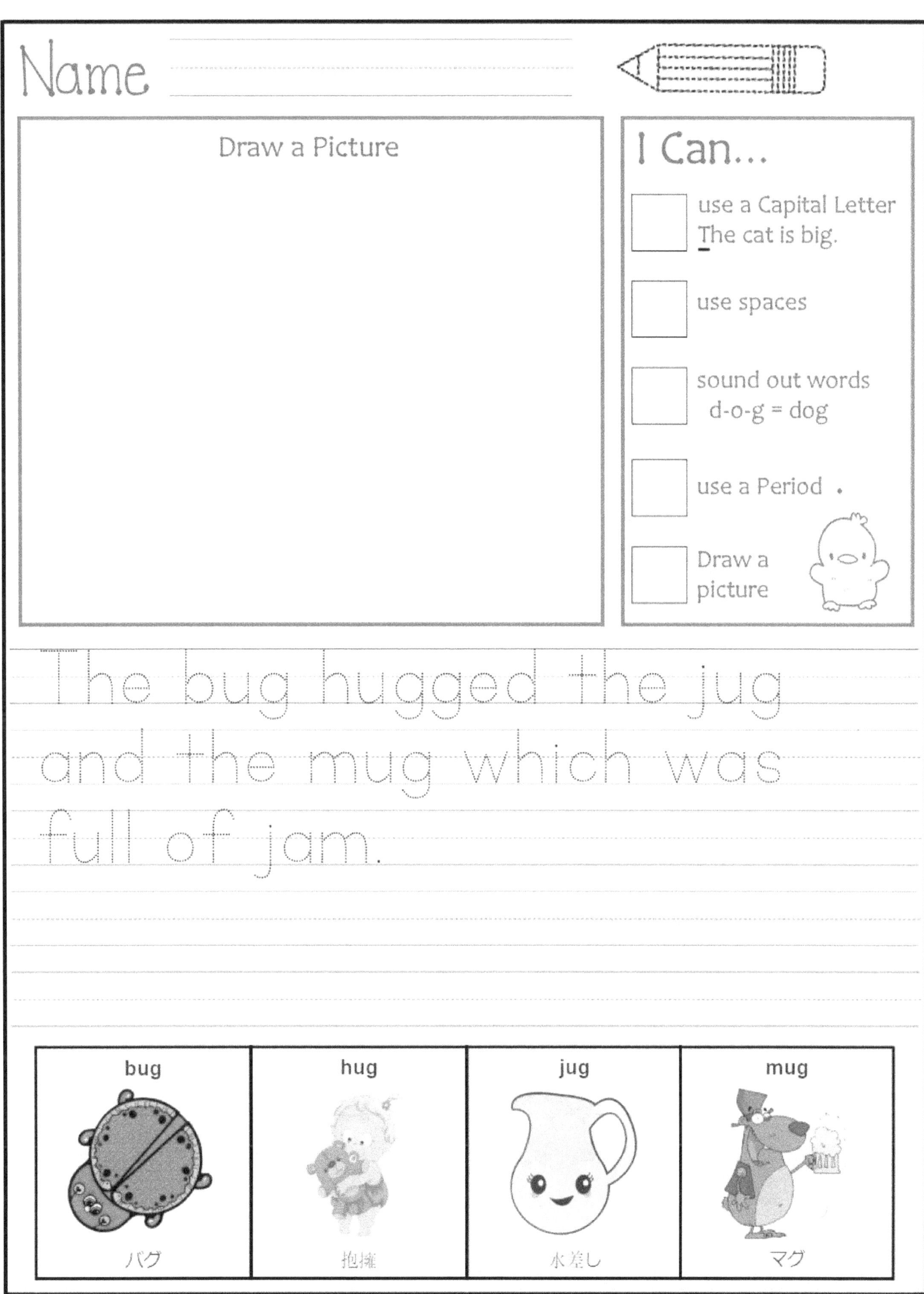

Name

Draw a Picture

I Can...

use a Capital Letter
The cat is big.

use spaces

sound out words
d-o-g = dog

use a Period .

Draw a
picture

The bug hugged the jug
and the mug which was
full of jam.

bug
バグ

hug
抱擁

jug
水差し

mug
マグ

Name: _______________ Date: _______________

Today is: [Monday] [Tuesday] [Wednesday]
[Thursday] [Friday]

Direction: Trace and read the sentences.

cot	dot	hot	pot
ベッド	ドット	ホット	ポット

This is my cot.

There are many dots.

It is very hot.

He has a plant pot.

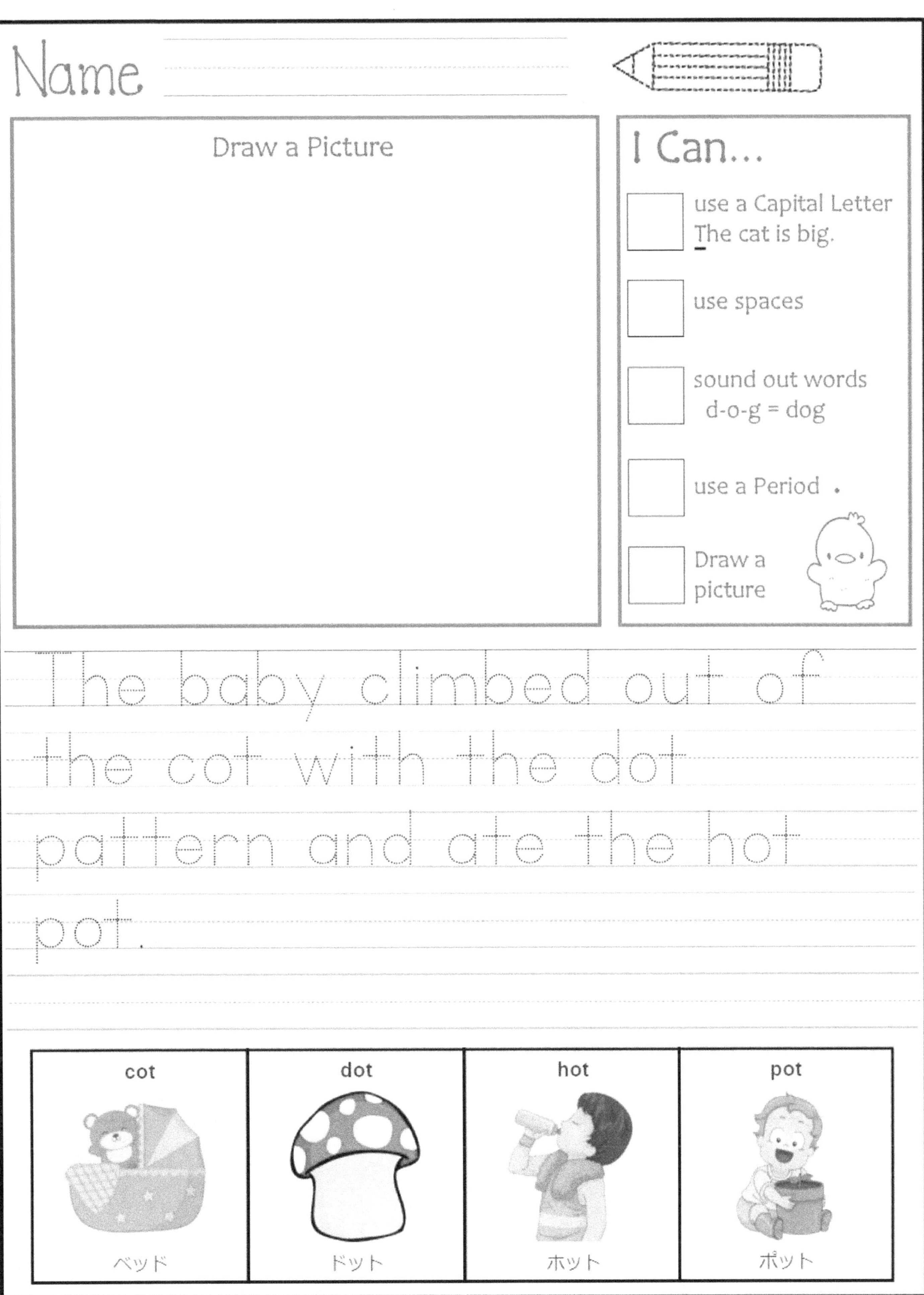

Name

Draw a Picture

I Can...

use a Capital Letter
The cat is big.

use spaces

sound out words
d-o-g = dog

use a Period .

Draw a
picture

The baby climbed out of
the cot with the dot
pattern and ate the hot
pot.

cot
ベッド

dot
ドット

hot
ホット

pot
ポット

Name: _________________ Date: _____________

Today is: | Monday | Tuesday | Wednesday |
| Thursday | Friday |

Direction: Read the words and make a sentence.

| **fun** | **gun** | **run** | **sun** |
| 楽しい | 銃 | 走る | 太陽 |

Name

Draw a Picture

I Can...

- [ ] use a Capital Letter
The cat is big.

- [ ] use spaces

- [ ] sound out words
d-o-g = dog

- [ ] use a Period .

- [ ] Draw a picture

Name: ______________________ Date: ______________________

Today is: Monday Tuesday Wednesday Thursday Friday

Name: _________________________ Date: _______________

Today is: [Monday] [Tuesday] [Wednesday]
[Thursday] [Friday]

Direction: Read the words and make a sentence.

bag	rag	tag	wag
バッグ	ぼろ	鬼ごっこ	振る

Name ____________________

Draw a Picture

I Can...

- ☐ use a Capital Letter
  The cat is big.

- ☐ use spaces

- ☐ sound out words
  d-o-g = dog

- ☐ use a Period .

- ☐ Draw a picture

Name: ________________   Date: ________________

Today is: [Monday] [Tuesday] [Wednesday]
[Thursday] [Friday]

Name: _______________ Date: _______________

Today is: [Monday] [Tuesday] [Wednesday]
[Thursday] [Friday]

Direction: Read the words and make a sentence.

can	man	pan	van
缶	おとこ	パン	バン

Name

Draw a Picture

I Can...

use a Capital Letter
The cat is big.

use spaces

sound out words
d-o-g = dog

use a Period .

Draw a
picture

Name: _________________ Date: _________________

Today is: Monday Tuesday Wednesday

Thursday Friday

Name: _______________________ Date: _______________________

Today is: Monday Tuesday Wednesday

Thursday Friday

Direction: Read the words and make a sentence.

cut	gut	hut	nut
切る	腸	小屋	ナット

Name ________________________

Draw a Picture

I Can...

- [ ] use a Capital Letter
  <u>T</u>he cat is big.

- [ ] use spaces

- [ ] sound out words
  d-o-g = dog

- [ ] use a Period .

- [ ] Draw a picture

Name: _______________________ Date: _______________________

Today is: Monday   Tuesday   Wednesday
           Thursday   Friday

Name: _______________________ Date: _______________

Today is: Monday   Tuesday   Wednesday

Thursday   Friday

Direction: Read the words and make a sentence.

fat	cat	hat	mat
太い	ネコ	帽子	マット

Name

Draw a Picture

I Can...

- [ ] use a Capital Letter
  The cat is big.

- [ ] use spaces

- [ ] sound out words
  d-o-g = dog

- [ ] use a Period .

- [ ] Draw a picture

Name: _______________________ Date: _______________

Today is: Monday   Tuesday   Wednesday

Thursday   Friday

Name: _________________ Date: _____________

Today is: Monday   Tuesday   Wednesday

Thursday   Friday

Direction: Read the words and make a sentence.

cab	lab	tab	crab
タクシー	ラボ	タブ	カニ

Name

Draw a Picture

I Can...

- [ ] use a Capital Letter
  The cat is big.

- [ ] use spaces

- [ ] sound out words
  d-o-g = dog

- [ ] use a Period .

- [ ] Draw a picture

Name: _______________________ Date: _______________________

Today is: Monday Tuesday Wednesday

Thursday Friday

Name: _______________ Date: _______________

Today is: Monday Tuesday Wednesday Thursday Friday

Direction: Read the words and make a sentence.

ham	jam	ram	clam
ハム	混雑する	羊	シェル

Name

Draw a Picture

I Can...

☐ use a Capital Letter
The cat is big.

☐ use spaces

☐ sound out words
d-o-g = dog

☐ use a Period .

☐ Draw a picture

Name: _______________________ Date: _______________________

Today is: Monday Tuesday Wednesday Thursday Friday

Name: _________________________ Date: _____________

Today is: [Monday] [Tuesday] [Wednesday]
           [Thursday] [Friday]

Direction: Read the words and make a sentence.

bed	led	red	wed
ベッド	主導	赤	結婚式

Name

Draw a Picture

I Can...

- [ ] use a Capital Letter
  The cat is big.

- [ ] use spaces

- [ ] sound out words
  d-o-g = dog

- [ ] use a Period .

- [ ] Draw a picture

Name: __________________   Date: __________

Today is: Monday   Tuesday   Wednesday

Thursday   Friday

Name: _______________________ Date: _______________

Today is: Monday | Tuesday | Wednesday | Thursday | Friday

Direction: Read the words and make a sentence.

bad	dad	mad	sad
悪い	パパ	狂った	悲しい

Name

Draw a Picture

I Can...

- [ ] use a Capital Letter
  <u>T</u>he cat is big.

- [ ] use spaces

- [ ] sound out words
  d-o-g = dog

- [ ] use a Period .

- [ ] Draw a picture

Name: _______________________   Date: _______________

Today is: [Monday] [Tuesday] [Wednesday]
           [Thursday] [Friday]

Name: _________________________ Date: _______________

Today is: [Monday] [Tuesday] [Wednesday]
[Thursday] [Friday]

Direction: Read the words and make a sentence.

den	hen	pen	ten
デン	編	厩舎	十

Name _______________________

Draw a Picture

I Can...

- ☐ use a Capital Letter
  <u>T</u>he cat is big.

- ☐ use spaces

- ☐ sound out words
  d-o-g = dog

- ☐ use a Period .

- ☐ Draw a picture

Name: _______________ Date: _______________

Today is: Monday Tuesday Wednesday

Thursday Friday

Name: ___________________ Date: ___________________

Today is: [Monday] [Tuesday] [Wednesday]
[Thursday] [Friday]

Direction: Read the words and make a sentence.

gum	mum	sum	drum
グミ	お母さん	和	ドラム

Name

Draw a Picture

I Can...

- [ ] use a Capital Letter
  The cat is big.

- [ ] use spaces

- [ ] sound out words
  d-o-g = dog

- [ ] use a Period .

- [ ] Draw a picture

Name: _______________________ Date: _______________________

Today is: Monday Tuesday Wednesday Thursday Friday

Name: _________________ Date: _____________

Today is: [Monday] [Tuesday] [Wednesday]
[Thursday] [Friday]

Direction: Read the words and make a sentence.

bid	hid	kid	lid
入札	隠す	キッド	蓋

Name _______________________

<table>
<tr><td>Draw a Picture</td><td>I Can...</td></tr>
</table>

Draw a Picture

I Can...

- [ ] use a Capital Letter
  <u>T</u>he cat is big.

- [ ] use spaces

- [ ] sound out words
  d-o-g = dog

- [ ] use a Period .

- [ ] Draw a picture

Name: _______________________ Date: _______________

Today is: Monday Tuesday Wednesday Thursday Friday

Direction: Read the words and make a sentence.

big	dig	pig	wig
大きい	掘る	豚	かつら

Name

Draw a Picture

I Can...

- [ ] use a Capital Letter
  <u>T</u>he cat is big.

- [ ] use spaces

- [ ] sound out words
  d-o-g = dog

- [ ] use a Period .

- [ ] Draw a picture

Name: _______________________ Date: _______________

Today is: Monday   Tuesday   Wednesday
          Thursday   Friday

Name: ____________________ Date: ____________________

Today is: Monday Tuesday Wednesday Thursday Friday

Direction: Read the words and make a sentence.

bin	fin	pin	win
	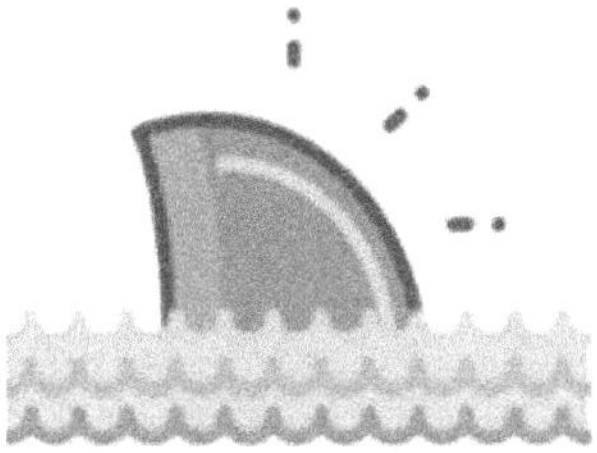		
置き場	フィン	ピン	勝つ

____

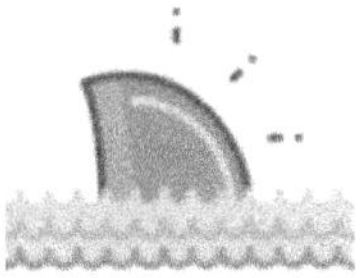

____

____

____

Name

Draw a Picture

I Can...

- [ ] use a Capital Letter
  <u>T</u>he cat is big.

- [ ] use spaces

- [ ] sound out words
  d-o-g = dog

- [ ] use a Period .

- [ ] Draw a picture

Name: _______________________ Date: _______________________

Today is: Monday   Tuesday   Wednesday

Thursday   Friday

Name: _________________________ Date: _________________________

Today is: [Monday] [Tuesday] [Wednesday]
[Thursday] [Friday]

Direction: Read the words and make a sentence.

hip	lip	nip	sip
ヒップ	唇	ニップ	ドリンク

Name

Draw a Picture

I Can...

- [ ] use a Capital Letter
  <u>T</u>he cat is big.

- [ ] use spaces

- [ ] sound out words
  d-o-g = dog

- [ ] use a Period .

- [ ] Draw a picture

Name: _______________________ Date: _______________

Today is: Monday Tuesday Wednesday Thursday Friday

Name: _______________________ Date: _______________________

Today is: [Monday] [Tuesday] [Wednesday]
[Thursday] [Friday]

Direction: Read the words and make a sentence.

fit	hit	kit	sit
フィット	ヒット	キット	座る

Name

Draw a Picture

I Can...

☐ use a Capital Letter
The cat is big.

☐ use spaces

☐ sound out words
d-o-g = dog

☐ use a Period .

☐ Draw a picture

Name: _______________   Date: _______________

Today is: Monday Tuesday Wednesday Thursday Friday

Name: _____________________   Date: _____________

Today is: [Monday] [Tuesday] [Wednesday]
[Thursday] [Friday]

Direction: Read the words and make a sentence.

cob	job	rob	sob
コーン	ジョブ	奪う	泣く

Name

Draw a Picture

I Can...

- [ ] use a Capital Letter
  The cat is big.

- [ ] use spaces

- [ ] sound out words
  d-o-g = dog

- [ ] use a Period .

- [ ] Draw a picture

Name: _______________________ Date: _______________

Today is: Monday Tuesday Wednesday Thursday Friday

Name: _________________________ Date: _______________

Today is: [Monday] [Tuesday] [Wednesday]
[Thursday] [Friday]

Direction: Read the words and make a sentence.

dog	hog	jog	log
犬	豚	ジョギング	木材

Name

Draw a Picture

I Can...

- [ ] use a Capital Letter
The cat is big.

- [ ] use spaces

- [ ] sound out words
d-o-g = dog

- [ ] use a Period .

- [ ] Draw a picture

Name: _____________________ Date: _____________

Today is: **Monday** **Tuesday** **Wednesday** **Thursday** **Friday**

Name: _________________ Date: _____________

Today is: Monday   Tuesday   Wednesday
           Thursday   Friday

Direction: Read the words and make a sentence.

bug	hug	jug	mug
バグ	抱擁	水差し	マグ

Name ___________________________

<table>
<tr><td>Draw a Picture</td><td>## I Can...</td></tr>
</table>

Draw a Picture

I Can...

☐ use a Capital Letter
The cat is big.

☐ use spaces

☐ sound out words
d-o-g = dog

☐ use a Period .

☐ Draw a picture

Name: _______________________ Date: _______________________

Today is: Monday Tuesday Wednesday Thursday Friday

Name: _________________________ Date: _______________

Today is: Monday   Tuesday   Wednesday

Thursday   Friday

Direction: Read the words and make a sentence.

cot	dot	hot	pot
ベッド	ドット	ホット	ポット

Name

Draw a Picture

I Can...

- [ ] use a Capital Letter
  <u>T</u>he cat is big.

- [ ] use spaces

- [ ] sound out words
  d-o-g = dog

- [ ] use a Period .

- [ ] Draw a picture

Name: __________________   Date: __________________

Today is: Monday   Tuesday   Wednesday

Thursday   Friday